GW01312837

DOG WALKING JOURNAL

CASE OF EMERGENCY

WALKER DETAILS

OWNER NAME	
FULL ADDRESS	
EMAIL & NUMBER	
EMERGENCY CONTACT	
EMERGENCY NUMBER	
DOCTOR DETAILS	

INCIDENT DETAILS

If found please return this

DOG WALKING
JOURNAL

to:

_____

_____

LOCATION		DATE
START POINT		
END POINT		/ /

NO. OF DOGS WALKED		WALK RATING	1	2	3	4	5
WEATHER CONDITION	☀ ☁ ❄ ⛈ 〜	TIME OF YEAR	🌷	☀	🍂	❄

WALK START	🕐	DOG WALK CHECKLIST	
WALK END		☐ WASTE BAG	☐ TREAT POUCH
TOTAL WALK	↻	☐ DOG LEASH	☐ WHISTLE
		☐ WATER BOWL	☐ GLOW COLLAR

DOG NAMES & OWNERS

POOP LOG

ROUTE TAKEN	REST STOPS & FOOD

FURTHER NOTES & OBSERVATIONS

LOCATION		DATE				
START POINT						
END POINT						

NO. OF DOGS WALKED		WALK RATING	1	2	3	4	5
WEATHER CONDITION	☀ ☁ ❄ ⛈ 🌬	TIME OF YEAR	🌷 ☀ 🍃 ❄				

WALK START	🕐	**DOG WALK CHECKLIST**	
WALK END		☐ WASTE BAG	☐ TREAT POUCH
TOTAL WALK	🔄	☐ DOG LEASH	☐ WHISTLE
		☐ WATER BOWL	☐ GLOW COLLAR

DOG NAMES & OWNERS

POOP LOG

ROUTE TAKEN | REST STOPS & FOOD

ROUTE TAKEN	REST STOPS & FOOD

FURTHER NOTES & OBSERVATIONS

LOCATION		DATE
START POINT		
END POINT		/ /

NO. OF DOGS WALKED		WALK RATING	1	2	3	4	5

WEATHER CONDITION	☀ ☁ ❄ ⛈ 🌬	TIME OF YEAR	🌷 ☀ 🍃 ❄

WALK START		DOG WALK CHECKLIST	
WALK END		☐ WASTE BAG	☐ TREAT POUCH
TOTAL WALK		☐ DOG LEASH	☐ WHISTLE
		☐ WATER BOWL	☐ GLOW COLLAR

DOG NAMES & OWNERS

POOP LOG

ROUTE TAKEN | REST STOPS & FOOD

ROUTE TAKEN	REST STOPS & FOOD

FURTHER NOTES & OBSERVATIONS

LOCATION		DATE				
START POINT						
END POINT		/ /				

NO. OF DOGS WALKED		WALK RATING	1	2	3	4	5
WEATHER CONDITION	☀ ☁ ❄ ⚡ 〰	TIME OF YEAR	🌷	☀	🍂	❄	

WALK START	🕐	**DOG WALK CHECKLIST**	
WALK END		☐ WASTE BAG	☐ TREAT POUCH
TOTAL WALK	🔄	☐ DOG LEASH	☐ WHISTLE
		☐ WATER BOWL	☐ GLOW COLLAR

DOG NAMES & OWNERS

POOP LOG

ROUTE TAKEN	REST STOPS & FOOD

FURTHER NOTES & OBSERVATIONS

LOCATION		DATE	
START POINT			
END POINT		/ /	

NO. OF DOGS WALKED		WALK RATING	1	2	3	4	5
WEATHER CONDITION	☀ ☁ ❄ ⛈ 💨	TIME OF YEAR	🌷 ☀ 🍁 ❄				

WALK START	🕐	**DOG WALK CHECKLIST**	
WALK END		☐ WASTE BAG ☐ TREAT POUCH	
TOTAL WALK	🔄	☐ DOG LEASH ☐ WHISTLE	
		☐ WATER BOWL ☐ GLOW COLLAR	

DOG NAMES & OWNERS

POOP LOG

ROUTE TAKEN | REST STOPS & FOOD

ROUTE TAKEN	REST STOPS & FOOD

FURTHER NOTES & OBSERVATIONS

LOCATION		DATE	
START POINT			
END POINT			

NO. OF DOGS WALKED		WALK RATING	1	2	3	4	5
WEATHER CONDITION	☀ ☁ ❄ ⛈ 🌬	TIME OF YEAR	🌷 ☀ 🍂 ❄				

WALK START	🕐	DOG WALK CHECKLIST	
WALK END		☐ WASTE BAG	☐ TREAT POUCH
TOTAL WALK	🔄	☐ DOG LEASH	☐ WHISTLE
		☐ WATER BOWL	☐ GLOW COLLAR

DOG NAMES & OWNERS

POOP LOG

ROUTE TAKEN | REST STOPS & FOOD

ROUTE TAKEN	REST STOPS & FOOD

FURTHER NOTES & OBSERVATIONS

LOCATION		DATE
START POINT		
END POINT		/ /

NO. OF DOGS WALKED		WALK RATING	1	2	3	4	5
WEATHER CONDITION	☀ ☁ ❄ ⛈ 🌬	TIME OF YEAR	🌷 ☀ 🍃 ❄				

WALK START		DOG WALK CHECKLIST	
WALK END	🕐	☐ WASTE BAG	☐ TREAT POUCH
TOTAL WALK	○	☐ DOG LEASH	☐ WHISTLE
		☐ WATER BOWL	☐ GLOW COLLAR

DOG NAMES & OWNERS

POOP LOG

ROUTE TAKEN / REST STOPS & FOOD

ROUTE TAKEN	REST STOPS & FOOD

FURTHER NOTES & OBSERVATIONS

LOCATION		DATE	
START POINT			
END POINT			

NO. OF DOGS WALKED		WALK RATING	1	2	3	4	5
WEATHER CONDITION	☀ ☁ ❄ ⛈ 〰	TIME OF YEAR	🌷 ☀ 🍃 ❄

WALK START		**DOG WALK CHECKLIST**	
WALK END	⊕	☐ WASTE BAG ☐ TREAT POUCH	
TOTAL WALK	◯	☐ DOG LEASH ☐ WHISTLE	
		☐ WATER BOWL ☐ GLOW COLLAR	

DOG NAMES & OWNERS

POOP LOG

ROUTE TAKEN	REST STOPS & FOOD

FURTHER NOTES & OBSERVATIONS

LOCATION		DATE	
START POINT			
END POINT			

NO. OF DOGS WALKED		WALK RATING	1	2	3	4	5
WEATHER CONDITION	☀ ☁ ❄ ⚡ 💨	TIME OF YEAR	🌷	☀	🍃	❄	

WALK START		DOG WALK CHECKLIST	
WALK END		☐ WASTE BAG	☐ TREAT POUCH
TOTAL WALK		☐ DOG LEASH	☐ WHISTLE
		☐ WATER BOWL	☐ GLOW COLLAR

DOG NAMES & OWNERS

POOP LOG

ROUTE TAKEN	REST STOPS & FOOD

FURTHER NOTES & OBSERVATIONS

LOCATION		DATE	
START POINT			
END POINT			

NO. OF DOGS WALKED		WALK RATING	1 2 3 4 5
WEATHER CONDITION	☀ ☁ ❄ ⛈ 🌬	TIME OF YEAR	🌷 ☀ 🍃 ❄

WALK START	🕐	DOG WALK CHECKLIST	
WALK END		☐ WASTE BAG ☐ TREAT POUCH	
TOTAL WALK	🔄	☐ DOG LEASH ☐ WHISTLE	
		☐ WATER BOWL ☐ GLOW COLLAR	

DOG NAMES & OWNERS

POOP LOG

ROUTE TAKEN | REST STOPS & FOOD

FURTHER NOTES & OBSERVATIONS

LOCATION		DATE		
START POINT				
END POINT		/	/	

NO. OF DOGS WALKED		WALK RATING	1	2	3	4	5
WEATHER CONDITION	☀ ☁ ❄ ⚡ 〰	TIME OF YEAR	🌷 ☀ 🍂 ❄				

WALK START		DOG WALK CHECKLIST	
WALK END		☐ WASTE BAG	☐ TREAT POUCH
TOTAL WALK		☐ DOG LEASH	☐ WHISTLE
		☐ WATER BOWL	☐ GLOW COLLAR

DOG NAMES & OWNERS

POOP LOG

ROUTE TAKEN | REST STOPS & FOOD

ROUTE TAKEN	REST STOPS & FOOD

FURTHER NOTES & OBSERVATIONS

LOCATION		DATE
START POINT		
END POINT		

NO. OF DOGS WALKED		WALK RATING	1	2	3	4	5
WEATHER CONDITION		TIME OF YEAR					

WALK START		DOG WALK CHECKLIST	
WALK END		☐ WASTE BAG	☐ TREAT POUCH
TOTAL WALK		☐ DOG LEASH	☐ WHISTLE
		☐ WATER BOWL	☐ GLOW COLLAR

DOG NAMES & OWNERS

POOP LOG

ROUTE TAKEN | REST STOPS & FOOD

ROUTE TAKEN	REST STOPS & FOOD

FURTHER NOTES & OBSERVATIONS

LOCATION		DATE
START POINT		
END POINT		/ /

NO. OF DOGS WALKED		WALK RATING	1	2	3	4	5
WEATHER CONDITION	☀ ☁ ❄ ⛈ 🌬	TIME OF YEAR	🌷 ☀ 🍃 ❄

WALK START	🕐	DOG WALK CHECKLIST

WALK END

☐ WASTE BAG ☐ TREAT POUCH

| TOTAL WALK | 🔄 |

☐ DOG LEASH ☐ WHISTLE

☐ WATER BOWL ☐ GLOW COLLAR

DOG NAMES & OWNERS

POOP LOG

ROUTE TAKEN | REST STOPS & FOOD

FURTHER NOTES & OBSERVATIONS

LOCATION		DATE
START POINT		
END POINT		

NO. OF DOGS WALKED		WALK RATING	1	2	3	4	5
WEATHER CONDITION	☀ ☁ ❄ ⛈ 🌬	TIME OF YEAR	🌷 ☀ 🍃 ❄				

WALK START		**DOG WALK CHECKLIST**	
WALK END		☐ WASTE BAG	☐ TREAT POUCH
TOTAL WALK		☐ DOG LEASH	☐ WHISTLE
		☐ WATER BOWL	☐ GLOW COLLAR

DOG NAMES & OWNERS

POOP LOG

ROUTE TAKEN	REST STOPS & FOOD

FURTHER NOTES & OBSERVATIONS

LOCATION		DATE	
START POINT			
END POINT		/ /	

NO. OF DOGS WALKED		WALK RATING	1	2	3	4	5
WEATHER CONDITION	☀ ☁ ❄ ⛈ 🌬	TIME OF YEAR	🌷 ☀ 🍃 ❄				

WALK START			DOG WALK CHECKLIST	
WALK END			☐ WASTE BAG	☐ TREAT POUCH
TOTAL WALK			☐ DOG LEASH	☐ WHISTLE
			☐ WATER BOWL	☐ GLOW COLLAR

DOG NAMES & OWNERS

POOP LOG

ROUTE TAKEN | REST STOPS & FOOD

ROUTE TAKEN	REST STOPS & FOOD

FURTHER NOTES & OBSERVATIONS

LOCATION		DATE			
START POINT					
END POINT					

NO. OF DOGS WALKED		WALK RATING	1	2	3	4	5
WEATHER CONDITION	☀ ☁ ❄ ⚡ 🌬	TIME OF YEAR	🌷 ☀ 🍃 ❄				

WALK START		DOG WALK CHECKLIST	
WALK END		☐ WASTE BAG	☐ TREAT POUCH
TOTAL WALK		☐ DOG LEASH	☐ WHISTLE
		☐ WATER BOWL	☐ GLOW COLLAR

DOG NAMES & OWNERS

POOP LOG

ROUTE TAKEN / REST STOPS & FOOD

ROUTE TAKEN	REST STOPS & FOOD

FURTHER NOTES & OBSERVATIONS

LOCATION		DATE	
START POINT			
END POINT		/ /	

NO. OF DOGS WALKED		WALK RATING	1	2	3	4	5
WEATHER CONDITION	☀ ☁ ❄ ⚡ 〜	TIME OF YEAR	🌷 ☀ 🍃 ❄			

WALK START	🕐	DOG WALK CHECKLIST	
WALK END		☐ WASTE BAG	☐ TREAT POUCH
TOTAL WALK	↻	☐ DOG LEASH	☐ WHISTLE
		☐ WATER BOWL	☐ GLOW COLLAR

DOG NAMES & OWNERS

POOP LOG

ROUTE TAKEN	REST STOPS & FOOD

FURTHER NOTES & OBSERVATIONS

LOCATION		DATE	
START POINT			
END POINT			

NO. OF DOGS WALKED		WALK RATING	1	2	3	4	5
WEATHER CONDITION	☀ ☁ ❄ ⚡ 💨	TIME OF YEAR	🌷 ☀ 🍂 ❄				

WALK START		DOG WALK CHECKLIST	
WALK END		☐ WASTE BAG	☐ TREAT POUCH
TOTAL WALK		☐ DOG LEASH	☐ WHISTLE
		☐ WATER BOWL	☐ GLOW COLLAR

DOG NAMES & OWNERS

POOP LOG

ROUTE TAKEN	REST STOPS & FOOD

FURTHER NOTES & OBSERVATIONS

LOCATION		DATE
START POINT		
END POINT		/ /

NO. OF DOGS WALKED		WALK RATING	1	2	3	4	5
WEATHER CONDITION	☀ ☁ ❄ ⛈ 🌬	TIME OF YEAR	🌷	☀	🍂	❄	

WALK START	🕐	DOG WALK CHECKLIST	
WALK END		☐ WASTE BAG	☐ TREAT POUCH
TOTAL WALK	◯	☐ DOG LEASH	☐ WHISTLE
		☐ WATER BOWL	☐ GLOW COLLAR

DOG NAMES & OWNERS

POOP LOG

ROUTE TAKEN | REST STOPS & FOOD

FURTHER NOTES & OBSERVATIONS

LOCATION		DATE
START POINT		
END POINT		

NO. OF DOGS WALKED		WALK RATING	1	2	3	4	5

WEATHER CONDITION	☀ ☁ ❄ ⛈ 💨	TIME OF YEAR	🌷 ☀ 🍂 ❄

WALK START		DOG WALK CHECKLIST
WALK END		☐ WASTE BAG ☐ TREAT POUCH
TOTAL WALK		☐ DOG LEASH ☐ WHISTLE
		☐ WATER BOWL ☐ GLOW COLLAR

DOG NAMES & OWNERS

POOP LOG

ROUTE TAKEN | REST STOPS & FOOD

FURTHER NOTES & OBSERVATIONS

LOCATION		DATE
START POINT		
END POINT		/ /

NO. OF DOGS WALKED		WALK RATING	1	2	3	4	5
WEATHER CONDITION	☀ ☁ ❄ ⛈ 🌬	TIME OF YEAR	🌷 ☀ 🍃 ❄				

WALK START		**DOG WALK CHECKLIST**	
WALK END		☐ WASTE BAG	☐ TREAT POUCH
TOTAL WALK		☐ DOG LEASH	☐ WHISTLE
		☐ WATER BOWL	☐ GLOW COLLAR

DOG NAMES & OWNERS

POOP LOG

ROUTE TAKEN / REST STOPS & FOOD

ROUTE TAKEN	REST STOPS & FOOD

FURTHER NOTES & OBSERVATIONS

LOCATION		DATE	
START POINT			
END POINT			

NO. OF DOGS WALKED		WALK RATING	1 2 3 4 5
WEATHER CONDITION	☀ ☁ ❄ ⛈ 🌬	TIME OF YEAR	🌷 ☀ 🍂 ❄

WALK START		DOG WALK CHECKLIST	
WALK END		☐ WASTE BAG	☐ TREAT POUCH
TOTAL WALK		☐ DOG LEASH	☐ WHISTLE
		☐ WATER BOWL	☐ GLOW COLLAR

DOG NAMES & OWNERS

POOP LOG

ROUTE TAKEN	REST STOPS & FOOD

FURTHER NOTES & OBSERVATIONS

LOCATION		DATE	
START POINT			
END POINT			

NO. OF DOGS WALKED		WALK RATING	1	2	3	4	5

WEATHER CONDITION	☀ ☁ ❄ ⚡ 〰	TIME OF YEAR	🌷 ☀ 🍃 ❄

WALK START		DOG WALK CHECKLIST	
WALK END		☐ WASTE BAG	☐ TREAT POUCH
TOTAL WALK		☐ DOG LEASH	☐ WHISTLE
		☐ WATER BOWL	☐ GLOW COLLAR

DOG NAMES & OWNERS

POOP LOG

ROUTE TAKEN | REST STOPS & FOOD

ROUTE TAKEN	REST STOPS & FOOD

FURTHER NOTES & OBSERVATIONS

LOCATION		DATE	
START POINT			
END POINT			

NO. OF DOGS WALKED		WALK RATING	1 2 3 4 5
WEATHER CONDITION	☀ ☁ ❄ ⛈ 〜	TIME OF YEAR	🌷 ☀ 🍃 ❄

WALK START		DOG WALK CHECKLIST	
WALK END		☐ WASTE BAG	☐ TREAT POUCH
TOTAL WALK		☐ DOG LEASH	☐ WHISTLE
		☐ WATER BOWL	☐ GLOW COLLAR

DOG NAMES & OWNERS

POOP LOG

ROUTE TAKEN	REST STOPS & FOOD

FURTHER NOTES & OBSERVATIONS

LOCATION		DATE				
START POINT						
END POINT		/ /				

NO. OF DOGS WALKED		WALK RATING	1	2	3	4	5
WEATHER CONDITION	☀ ☁ ❄ ⛈ 💨	TIME OF YEAR	🌷	☀	🍃	❄	

WALK START	🕐	DOG WALK CHECKLIST	
WALK END		☐ WASTE BAG ☐ TREAT POUCH	
TOTAL WALK	◯	☐ DOG LEASH ☐ WHISTLE	
		☐ WATER BOWL ☐ GLOW COLLAR	

DOG NAMES & OWNERS

POOP LOG

ROUTE TAKEN / REST STOPS & FOOD

ROUTE TAKEN	REST STOPS & FOOD

FURTHER NOTES & OBSERVATIONS

LOCATION		DATE
START POINT		
END POINT		

NO. OF DOGS WALKED		WALK RATING	1	2	3	4	5
WEATHER CONDITION	☀ ☁ ❄ ⛈ 🌬	TIME OF YEAR	🌷 ☀ 🍁 ❄				

WALK START		DOG WALK CHECKLIST	
WALK END		☐ WASTE BAG	☐ TREAT POUCH
TOTAL WALK		☐ DOG LEASH	☐ WHISTLE
		☐ WATER BOWL	☐ GLOW COLLAR

DOG NAMES & OWNERS

POOP LOG

ROUTE TAKEN & REST STOPS & FOOD

ROUTE TAKEN	REST STOPS & FOOD

FURTHER NOTES & OBSERVATIONS

LOCATION		DATE	
START POINT			
END POINT		/ /	

NO. OF DOGS WALKED		WALK RATING	1	2	3	4	5
WEATHER CONDITION	☀ ☁ ❄ ⛈ 🍃	TIME OF YEAR	🌷 ☀ 🍃 ❄				

WALK START	⏱	DOG WALK CHECKLIST	
WALK END		☐ WASTE BAG	☐ TREAT POUCH
TOTAL WALK	↻	☐ DOG LEASH	☐ WHISTLE
		☐ WATER BOWL	☐ GLOW COLLAR

DOG NAMES & OWNERS

POOP LOG

ROUTE TAKEN | REST STOPS & FOOD

ROUTE TAKEN	REST STOPS & FOOD

FURTHER NOTES & OBSERVATIONS

_____

LOCATION		DATE
START POINT		
END POINT		

NO. OF DOGS WALKED		WALK RATING	1	2	3	4	5
WEATHER CONDITION		TIME OF YEAR				

WALK START		DOG WALK CHECKLIST	
WALK END		☐ WASTE BAG	☐ TREAT POUCH
TOTAL WALK		☐ DOG LEASH	☐ WHISTLE
		☐ WATER BOWL	☐ GLOW COLLAR

DOG NAMES & OWNERS

POOP LOG

ROUTE TAKEN	REST STOPS & FOOD

FURTHER NOTES & OBSERVATIONS

LOCATION		DATE	
START POINT			
END POINT		/ /	

NO. OF DOGS WALKED		WALK RATING	1	2	3	4	5

WEATHER CONDITION	☀ ☁ ❄ ⚡ 〰	TIME OF YEAR	🌷 ☀ 🍃 ❄

WALK START	🕐	DOG WALK CHECKLIST	
WALK END		☐ WASTE BAG	☐ TREAT POUCH
TOTAL WALK	↻	☐ DOG LEASH	☐ WHISTLE
		☐ WATER BOWL	☐ GLOW COLLAR

DOG NAMES & OWNERS

POOP LOG

ROUTE TAKEN | REST STOPS & FOOD

ROUTE TAKEN	REST STOPS & FOOD

FURTHER NOTES & OBSERVATIONS

LOCATION		DATE
START POINT		
END POINT		

NO. OF DOGS WALKED		WALK RATING	1	2	3	4	5
WEATHER CONDITION		TIME OF YEAR				

WALK START		DOG WALK CHECKLIST	
WALK END		☐ WASTE BAG	☐ TREAT POUCH
TOTAL WALK		☐ DOG LEASH	☐ WHISTLE
		☐ WATER BOWL	☐ GLOW COLLAR

DOG NAMES & OWNERS

POOP LOG

ROUTE TAKEN / REST STOPS & FOOD

ROUTE TAKEN	REST STOPS & FOOD

FURTHER NOTES & OBSERVATIONS

LOCATION		DATE
START POINT		
END POINT		/ /

NO. OF DOGS WALKED		WALK RATING	1	2	3	4	5

WEATHER CONDITION	☀ ☁ ❄ ⛈ 💨	TIME OF YEAR	🌷 ☀ 🍃 ❄

WALK START	🕐	DOG WALK CHECKLIST
WALK END		☐ WASTE BAG ☐ TREAT POUCH
TOTAL WALK	↻	☐ DOG LEASH ☐ WHISTLE
		☐ WATER BOWL ☐ GLOW COLLAR

DOG NAMES & OWNERS

POOP LOG

ROUTE TAKEN | REST STOPS & FOOD

FURTHER NOTES & OBSERVATIONS

LOCATION		DATE	
START POINT			
END POINT			

NO. OF DOGS WALKED		WALK RATING	1	2	3	4	5
WEATHER CONDITION	☀ ☁ ❄ ⛈ 〰	TIME OF YEAR	🍃 ☀ 🍁 ❄

WALK START	🕐	DOG WALK CHECKLIST	
WALK END		☐ WASTE BAG ☐ TREAT POUCH	
TOTAL WALK	◯	☐ DOG LEASH ☐ WHISTLE	
		☐ WATER BOWL ☐ GLOW COLLAR	

DOG NAMES & OWNERS

POOP LOG

ROUTE TAKEN | REST STOPS & FOOD

ROUTE TAKEN	REST STOPS & FOOD

FURTHER NOTES & OBSERVATIONS

LOCATION		DATE	
START POINT			
END POINT		/ /	

NO. OF DOGS WALKED		WALK RATING	1 2 3 4 5
WEATHER CONDITION	☀ ☁ ❄ ⚡ 〜	TIME OF YEAR	🌷 ☀ 🍃 ❄

WALK START	🕐	DOG WALK CHECKLIST	
WALK END		☐ WASTE BAG	☐ TREAT POUCH
TOTAL WALK	↻	☐ DOG LEASH	☐ WHISTLE
		☐ WATER BOWL	☐ GLOW COLLAR

DOG NAMES & OWNERS

POOP LOG

ROUTE TAKEN	REST STOPS & FOOD

FURTHER NOTES & OBSERVATIONS

LOCATION		DATE
START POINT		
END POINT		

NO. OF DOGS WALKED		WALK RATING	1	2	3	4	5
WEATHER CONDITION		TIME OF YEAR				

WALK START		DOG WALK CHECKLIST	
WALK END		☐ WASTE BAG	☐ TREAT POUCH
TOTAL WALK		☐ DOG LEASH	☐ WHISTLE
		☐ WATER BOWL	☐ GLOW COLLAR

DOG NAMES & OWNERS

POOP LOG

ROUTE TAKEN · REST STOPS & FOOD

FURTHER NOTES & OBSERVATIONS

LOCATION		DATE		
START POINT				
END POINT		/	/	

NO. OF DOGS WALKED		WALK RATING	1	2	3	4	5

WEATHER CONDITION	☀ ☁ ❄ ⚡ 💨	TIME OF YEAR	🌷 ☀ 🍃 ❄

WALK START		**DOG WALK CHECKLIST**
WALK END		☐ WASTE BAG ☐ TREAT POUCH
TOTAL WALK		☐ DOG LEASH ☐ WHISTLE
		☐ WATER BOWL ☐ GLOW COLLAR

DOG NAMES & OWNERS

POOP LOG

ROUTE TAKEN | REST STOPS & FOOD

FURTHER NOTES & OBSERVATIONS

LOCATION		DATE		
START POINT				
END POINT				

NO. OF DOGS WALKED		WALK RATING	1	2	3	4	5
WEATHER CONDITION	☀ ☁ ❄ ⛈ 🌬	TIME OF YEAR	🌷 ☀ 🍃 ❄			

WALK START	🕐	**DOG WALK CHECKLIST**	
WALK END		☐ WASTE BAG	☐ TREAT POUCH
TOTAL WALK	🔄	☐ DOG LEASH	☐ WHISTLE
		☐ WATER BOWL	☐ GLOW COLLAR

DOG NAMES & OWNERS

POOP LOG

ROUTE TAKEN | REST STOPS & FOOD

ROUTE TAKEN	REST STOPS & FOOD

FURTHER NOTES & OBSERVATIONS

LOCATION		DATE
START POINT		
END POINT		/ /

NO. OF DOGS WALKED		WALK RATING	1 2 3 4 5
WEATHER CONDITION	☀ ☁ ❄ ⛈ 🌬	TIME OF YEAR	🌷 ☀ 🍃 ❄

WALK START	🕐	DOG WALK CHECKLIST	
WALK END		☐ WASTE BAG	☐ TREAT POUCH
TOTAL WALK	↻	☐ DOG LEASH	☐ WHISTLE
		☐ WATER BOWL	☐ GLOW COLLAR

DOG NAMES & OWNERS

POOP LOG

ROUTE TAKEN | REST STOPS & FOOD

ROUTE TAKEN	REST STOPS & FOOD

FURTHER NOTES & OBSERVATIONS

LOCATION		DATE	
START POINT			
END POINT			

NO. OF DOGS WALKED		WALK RATING	1	2	3	4	5
WEATHER CONDITION	☀ ☁ ❄ ⚡ 💨	TIME OF YEAR	🌷 ☀ 🍃 ❄				

WALK START	🕐	DOG WALK CHECKLIST	
WALK END		☐ WASTE BAG	☐ TREAT POUCH
TOTAL WALK	↻	☐ DOG LEASH	☐ WHISTLE
		☐ WATER BOWL	☐ GLOW COLLAR

DOG NAMES & OWNERS

POOP LOG

ROUTE TAKEN | REST STOPS & FOOD

ROUTE TAKEN	REST STOPS & FOOD

FURTHER NOTES & OBSERVATIONS

LOCATION		DATE	
START POINT			
END POINT		/ /	

NO. OF DOGS WALKED		WALK RATING	1 2 3 4 5
WEATHER CONDITION	☀ ☁ ❄ ⚡ 💨	TIME OF YEAR	🌷 ☀ 🍃 ❄

WALK START	🕐	DOG WALK CHECKLIST	
WALK END		☐ WASTE BAG	☐ TREAT POUCH
TOTAL WALK	🔄	☐ DOG LEASH	☐ WHISTLE
		☐ WATER BOWL	☐ GLOW COLLAR

DOG NAMES & OWNERS

POOP LOG

ROUTE TAKEN	REST STOPS & FOOD

FURTHER NOTES & OBSERVATIONS

LOCATION		DATE	
START POINT			
END POINT			

NO. OF DOGS WALKED		WALK RATING	1 2 3 4 5
WEATHER CONDITION	☀ ☁ ❄ ⛈ 🌬	TIME OF YEAR	🌷 ☀ 🍃 ❄

WALK START	🕐	**DOG WALK CHECKLIST**	
WALK END		☐ WASTE BAG ☐ TREAT POUCH	
TOTAL WALK	🔄	☐ DOG LEASH ☐ WHISTLE	
		☐ WATER BOWL ☐ GLOW COLLAR	

DOG NAMES & OWNERS

POOP LOG

ROUTE TAKEN	REST STOPS & FOOD

FURTHER NOTES & OBSERVATIONS

LOCATION		DATE	
START POINT			
END POINT		/ /	

NO. OF DOGS WALKED		WALK RATING	1 2 3 4 5

WEATHER CONDITION	☀ ☁ ❄ ⚡ 〰	TIME OF YEAR	🌷 ☀ 🍃 ❄

WALK START	🕐	DOG WALK CHECKLIST	
WALK END		☐ WASTE BAG	☐ TREAT POUCH
TOTAL WALK	↻	☐ DOG LEASH	☐ WHISTLE
		☐ WATER BOWL	☐ GLOW COLLAR

DOG NAMES & OWNERS

POOP LOG

ROUTE TAKEN	REST STOPS & FOOD

FURTHER NOTES & OBSERVATIONS

LOCATION		DATE	
START POINT			
END POINT			

NO. OF DOGS WALKED		WALK RATING	1	2	3	4	5
WEATHER CONDITION	☀ ☁ ❄ ⚡ 〰	TIME OF YEAR	🌷 ☀ 🍃 ❄				

WALK START	🕐		DOG WALK CHECKLIST	
WALK END			☐ WASTE BAG	☐ TREAT POUCH
TOTAL WALK	⟳		☐ DOG LEASH	☐ WHISTLE
			☐ WATER BOWL	☐ GLOW COLLAR

DOG NAMES & OWNERS

POOP LOG

ROUTE TAKEN | REST STOPS & FOOD

ROUTE TAKEN	REST STOPS & FOOD

FURTHER NOTES & OBSERVATIONS

LOCATION		DATE
START POINT		
END POINT		/ /

NO. OF DOGS WALKED		WALK RATING	1	2	3	4	5
WEATHER CONDITION		TIME OF YEAR				

WALK START		DOG WALK CHECKLIST	
WALK END		☐ WASTE BAG	☐ TREAT POUCH
TOTAL WALK		☐ DOG LEASH	☐ WHISTLE
		☐ WATER BOWL	☐ GLOW COLLAR

DOG NAMES & OWNERS

POOP LOG

ROUTE TAKEN	REST STOPS & FOOD

FURTHER NOTES & OBSERVATIONS

LOCATION		DATE
START POINT		
END POINT		/ /

NO. OF DOGS WALKED		WALK RATING	1 2 3 4 5
WEATHER CONDITION		TIME OF YEAR	

WALK START		DOG WALK CHECKLIST	
WALK END		☐ WASTE BAG	☐ TREAT POUCH
TOTAL WALK		☐ DOG LEASH	☐ WHISTLE
		☐ WATER BOWL	☐ GLOW COLLAR

DOG NAMES & OWNERS

POOP LOG

ROUTE TAKEN / REST STOPS & FOOD

FURTHER NOTES & OBSERVATIONS

LOCATION		DATE
START POINT		
END POINT		/ /

NO. OF DOGS WALKED		WALK RATING	1	2	3	4	5
WEATHER CONDITION	☀ ☁ ❄ ⚡ 🌬	TIME OF YEAR	🌷 ☀ 🍃 ❄			

WALK START	🕐	DOG WALK CHECKLIST	
WALK END		☐ WASTE BAG	☐ TREAT POUCH
TOTAL WALK	↻	☐ DOG LEASH	☐ WHISTLE
		☐ WATER BOWL	☐ GLOW COLLAR

DOG NAMES & OWNERS

POOP LOG

ROUTE TAKEN | REST STOPS & FOOD

ROUTE TAKEN	REST STOPS & FOOD

FURTHER NOTES & OBSERVATIONS

LOCATION		DATE	
START POINT			
END POINT			

NO. OF DOGS WALKED		WALK RATING	1	2	3	4	5
WEATHER CONDITION	☀ ☁ ❄ ⚡ 〰	TIME OF YEAR	🌷 ☀ 🍁 ❄				

WALK START	🕐	DOG WALK CHECKLIST	
WALK END		☐ WASTE BAG	☐ TREAT POUCH
TOTAL WALK	↻	☐ DOG LEASH	☐ WHISTLE
		☐ WATER BOWL	☐ GLOW COLLAR

DOG NAMES & OWNERS

POOP LOG

ROUTE TAKEN	REST STOPS & FOOD

FURTHER NOTES & OBSERVATIONS

LOCATION		DATE	
START POINT			
END POINT		/ /	

NO. OF DOGS WALKED		WALK RATING	1 2 3 4 5
WEATHER CONDITION	☀ ☁ ❄ ⚡ 〜	TIME OF YEAR	🌷 ☀ 🍃 ❄

WALK START	🕐	DOG WALK CHECKLIST	
WALK END		☐ WASTE BAG	☐ TREAT POUCH
TOTAL WALK	↻	☐ DOG LEASH	☐ WHISTLE
		☐ WATER BOWL	☐ GLOW COLLAR

DOG NAMES & OWNERS

POOP LOG

ROUTE TAKEN	REST STOPS & FOOD

FURTHER NOTES & OBSERVATIONS

LOCATION		DATE	
START POINT			
END POINT			

NO. OF DOGS WALKED		WALK RATING	1	2	3	4	5

WEATHER CONDITION	☀ ☁ ❄ ⚡ 〰	TIME OF YEAR	🌷 ☀ 🍁 ❄

WALK START		DOG WALK CHECKLIST	
WALK END		☐ WASTE BAG	☐ TREAT POUCH
TOTAL WALK		☐ DOG LEASH	☐ WHISTLE
		☐ WATER BOWL	☐ GLOW COLLAR

DOG NAMES & OWNERS

POOP LOG

ROUTE TAKEN	REST STOPS & FOOD

FURTHER NOTES & OBSERVATIONS

LOCATION		DATE	
START POINT			
END POINT		/ /	

NO. OF DOGS WALKED		WALK RATING	1 2 3 4 5
WEATHER CONDITION	☀ ☁ ❄ ⚡ ≈	TIME OF YEAR	❀ ☀ 🍃 ❄

WALK START	🕐	**DOG WALK CHECKLIST**	
WALK END		☐ WASTE BAG ☐ TREAT POUCH	
TOTAL WALK	↻	☐ DOG LEASH ☐ WHISTLE	
		☐ WATER BOWL ☐ GLOW COLLAR	

DOG NAMES & OWNERS

POOP LOG

ROUTE TAKEN / REST STOPS & FOOD

ROUTE TAKEN	REST STOPS & FOOD

FURTHER NOTES & OBSERVATIONS

LOCATION		DATE			
START POINT					
END POINT					

NO. OF DOGS WALKED		WALK RATING	1	2	3	4	5
WEATHER CONDITION	☀ ☁ ❄ ⛈ 🌬	TIME OF YEAR	🌷	☀	🍁	❄

WALK START	⏱	DOG WALK CHECKLIST	
WALK END		☐ WASTE BAG	☐ TREAT POUCH
TOTAL WALK	⭕	☐ DOG LEASH	☐ WHISTLE
		☐ WATER BOWL	☐ GLOW COLLAR

DOG NAMES & OWNERS

POOP LOG

ROUTE TAKEN	REST STOPS & FOOD

FURTHER NOTES & OBSERVATIONS

LOCATION		DATE	
START POINT			
END POINT		/ /	

NO. OF DOGS WALKED		WALK RATING	1 2 3 4 5
WEATHER CONDITION	☀ ☁ ❄ ⛈ 🌬	TIME OF YEAR	🌷 ☀ 🍃 ❄

WALK START		DOG WALK CHECKLIST	
WALK END	🕐	☐ WASTE BAG	☐ TREAT POUCH
TOTAL WALK	🔄	☐ DOG LEASH	☐ WHISTLE
		☐ WATER BOWL	☐ GLOW COLLAR

DOG NAMES & OWNERS

POOP LOG

ROUTE TAKEN | REST STOPS & FOOD

ROUTE TAKEN	REST STOPS & FOOD

FURTHER NOTES & OBSERVATIONS

LOCATION		DATE	
START POINT			
END POINT			

NO. OF DOGS WALKED		WALK RATING	1	2	3	4	5
WEATHER CONDITION	☀ ☁ ❄ ⚡ 🌬	TIME OF YEAR	🌷 ☀ 🍃 ❄				

WALK START	🕐	**DOG WALK CHECKLIST**	
WALK END		☐ WASTE BAG	☐ TREAT POUCH
TOTAL WALK	🔄	☐ DOG LEASH	☐ WHISTLE
		☐ WATER BOWL	☐ GLOW COLLAR

DOG NAMES & OWNERS

POOP LOG

ROUTE TAKEN | REST STOPS & FOOD

ROUTE TAKEN	REST STOPS & FOOD

FURTHER NOTES & OBSERVATIONS

LOCATION		DATE	
START POINT			
END POINT		/ /	

NO. OF DOGS WALKED		WALK RATING	1 2 3 4 5
WEATHER CONDITION	☀ ☁ ❄ ⚡ 🌬	TIME OF YEAR	🌷 ☀ 🍃 ❄

WALK START	🕐	DOG WALK CHECKLIST	
WALK END		☐ WASTE BAG ☐ TREAT POUCH	
TOTAL WALK	⟳	☐ DOG LEASH ☐ WHISTLE	
		☐ WATER BOWL ☐ GLOW COLLAR	

DOG NAMES & OWNERS

POOP LOG

ROUTE TAKEN / REST STOPS & FOOD

ROUTE TAKEN	REST STOPS & FOOD

FURTHER NOTES & OBSERVATIONS

LOCATION		DATE			
START POINT					
END POINT		/	/		

NO. OF DOGS WALKED		WALK RATING	1	2	3	4	5
WEATHER CONDITION	☀ ☁ ❄ ⚡ 🌬	TIME OF YEAR	🌷 ☀ 🍁 ❄				

WALK START		DOG WALK CHECKLIST	
WALK END		☐ WASTE BAG	☐ TREAT POUCH
TOTAL WALK		☐ DOG LEASH	☐ WHISTLE
		☐ WATER BOWL	☐ GLOW COLLAR

DOG NAMES & OWNERS

POOP LOG

ROUTE TAKEN	REST STOPS & FOOD

FURTHER NOTES & OBSERVATIONS

LOCATION		DATE		
START POINT				
END POINT		/	/	

NO. OF DOGS WALKED		WALK RATING	1	2	3	4	5
WEATHER CONDITION	☀ ☁ ❄ ⛈ 🌬	TIME OF YEAR	🌷	☀	🍃	❄	

WALK START	🕐	DOG WALK CHECKLIST	
WALK END		☐ WASTE BAG ☐ TREAT POUCH	
TOTAL WALK	◯	☐ DOG LEASH ☐ WHISTLE	
		☐ WATER BOWL ☐ GLOW COLLAR	

DOG NAMES & OWNERS

POOP LOG

ROUTE TAKEN | REST STOPS & FOOD

FURTHER NOTES & OBSERVATIONS

LOCATION		DATE				
START POINT						
END POINT		/ /				

NO. OF DOGS WALKED		WALK RATING	1	2	3	4	5
WEATHER CONDITION	☀ ☁ ❄ ⚡ 💨	TIME OF YEAR	🌷 ☀ 🍃 ❄				

WALK START	🕐	**DOG WALK CHECKLIST**	
WALK END		☐ WASTE BAG	☐ TREAT POUCH
TOTAL WALK	⟳	☐ DOG LEASH	☐ WHISTLE
		☐ WATER BOWL	☐ GLOW COLLAR

DOG NAMES & OWNERS

POOP LOG

ROUTE TAKEN	REST STOPS & FOOD

FURTHER NOTES & OBSERVATIONS

LOCATION		DATE	
START POINT			
END POINT		/ /	

NO. OF DOGS WALKED		WALK RATING	1 2 3 4 5
WEATHER CONDITION	☀ ☁ ❄ ⚡ 〜	TIME OF YEAR	🌷 ☀ 🍂 ❄

WALK START	🕐	DOG WALK CHECKLIST
WALK END		☐ WASTE BAG ☐ TREAT POUCH
TOTAL WALK	🔄	☐ DOG LEASH ☐ WHISTLE
		☐ WATER BOWL ☐ GLOW COLLAR

DOG NAMES & OWNERS

POOP LOG

ROUTE TAKEN | REST STOPS & FOOD

ROUTE TAKEN	REST STOPS & FOOD

FURTHER NOTES & OBSERVATIONS

LOCATION		DATE
START POINT		
END POINT		

NO. OF DOGS WALKED		WALK RATING	1	2	3	4	5

WEATHER CONDITION	☀ ☁ ❄ ⛈ 🌬	TIME OF YEAR	🌷 ☀ 🍃 ❄

WALK START	🕐	**DOG WALK CHECKLIST**
WALK END		☐ WASTE BAG ☐ TREAT POUCH
TOTAL WALK	↻	☐ DOG LEASH ☐ WHISTLE
		☐ WATER BOWL ☐ GLOW COLLAR

DOG NAMES & OWNERS

POOP LOG

ROUTE TAKEN / REST STOPS & FOOD

ROUTE TAKEN	REST STOPS & FOOD

FURTHER NOTES & OBSERVATIONS

LOCATION		DATE
START POINT		
END POINT		/ /

NO. OF DOGS WALKED		WALK RATING	1	2	3	4	5
WEATHER CONDITION	☀ ☁ ❄ ⚡ 🌬	TIME OF YEAR	🌷 ☀ 🍃 ❄				

WALK START	🕐	DOG WALK CHECKLIST	
WALK END		☐ WASTE BAG	☐ TREAT POUCH
TOTAL WALK	⭮	☐ DOG LEASH	☐ WHISTLE
		☐ WATER BOWL	☐ GLOW COLLAR

DOG NAMES & OWNERS

POOP LOG

ROUTE TAKEN	REST STOPS & FOOD

FURTHER NOTES & OBSERVATIONS

LOCATION		DATE
START POINT		
END POINT		

NO. OF DOGS WALKED		WALK RATING	1	2	3	4	5
WEATHER CONDITION	☀ ☁ ❄ ⛆ ≈	TIME OF YEAR	❀ ☀ 🍂 ❄				

WALK START		DOG WALK CHECKLIST	
WALK END		☐ WASTE BAG	☐ TREAT POUCH
TOTAL WALK		☐ DOG LEASH	☐ WHISTLE
		☐ WATER BOWL	☐ GLOW COLLAR

DOG NAMES & OWNERS

POOP LOG

ROUTE TAKEN | REST STOPS & FOOD

ROUTE TAKEN	REST STOPS & FOOD

FURTHER NOTES & OBSERVATIONS

LOCATION		DATE	
START POINT			
END POINT			

NO. OF DOGS WALKED		WALK RATING	1 2 3 4 5
WEATHER CONDITION	☀ ☁ ❄ ⛈ 🌬	TIME OF YEAR	🌷 ☀ 🍃 ❄

WALK START	🕐	**DOG WALK CHECKLIST**	
WALK END		☐ WASTE BAG	☐ TREAT POUCH
TOTAL WALK	↻	☐ DOG LEASH	☐ WHISTLE
		☐ WATER BOWL	☐ GLOW COLLAR

DOG NAMES & OWNERS

POOP LOG

ROUTE TAKEN / REST STOPS & FOOD

ROUTE TAKEN	REST STOPS & FOOD

FURTHER NOTES & OBSERVATIONS

LOCATION		DATE
START POINT		
END POINT		

NO. OF DOGS WALKED		WALK RATING	1	2	3	4	5
WEATHER CONDITION		TIME OF YEAR				

WALK START		DOG WALK CHECKLIST	
WALK END		☐ WASTE BAG	☐ TREAT POUCH
TOTAL WALK		☐ DOG LEASH	☐ WHISTLE
		☐ WATER BOWL	☐ GLOW COLLAR

DOG NAMES & OWNERS

POOP LOG

ROUTE TAKEN / REST STOPS & FOOD

ROUTE TAKEN	REST STOPS & FOOD

FURTHER NOTES & OBSERVATIONS

LOCATION		DATE	
START POINT			
END POINT		/ /	

NO. OF DOGS WALKED		WALK RATING	1	2	3	4	5
WEATHER CONDITION	☀ ☁ ❄ ⚡ 🌬	TIME OF YEAR	🌷 ☀ 🍃 ❄				

WALK START	🕐	**DOG WALK CHECKLIST**	
WALK END		☐ WASTE BAG ☐ TREAT POUCH	
TOTAL WALK	↻	☐ DOG LEASH ☐ WHISTLE	
		☐ WATER BOWL ☐ GLOW COLLAR	

DOG NAMES & OWNERS

POOP LOG

ROUTE TAKEN & REST STOPS & FOOD

ROUTE TAKEN	REST STOPS & FOOD

FURTHER NOTES & OBSERVATIONS

LOCATION		DATE	
START POINT			
END POINT		/ /	

NO. OF DOGS WALKED		WALK RATING	1 2 3 4 5
WEATHER CONDITION	☀ ☁ ❄ ⚡ 〰	TIME OF YEAR	🌷 ☀ 🍁 ❄

WALK START		DOG WALK CHECKLIST	
WALK END		☐ WASTE BAG	☐ TREAT POUCH
TOTAL WALK		☐ DOG LEASH	☐ WHISTLE
		☐ WATER BOWL	☐ GLOW COLLAR

DOG NAMES & OWNERS

POOP LOG

ROUTE TAKEN	REST STOPS & FOOD

FURTHER NOTES & OBSERVATIONS

LOCATION		DATE
START POINT		
END POINT		/ /

NO. OF DOGS WALKED		WALK RATING	1	2	3	4	5
WEATHER CONDITION	☀ ☁ ❄ ⛈ 🌬	TIME OF YEAR	🌷	☀	🍃	❄	

WALK START		**DOG WALK CHECKLIST**	
WALK END	⏱	☐ WASTE BAG	☐ TREAT POUCH
TOTAL WALK	🔄	☐ DOG LEASH	☐ WHISTLE
		☐ WATER BOWL	☐ GLOW COLLAR

DOG NAMES & OWNERS

POOP LOG

ROUTE TAKEN	REST STOPS & FOOD

FURTHER NOTES & OBSERVATIONS

LOCATION		DATE
START POINT		
END POINT		

NO. OF DOGS WALKED		WALK RATING	1	2	3	4	5
WEATHER CONDITION	☀ ☁ ❄ ⛈ 💨	TIME OF YEAR	🌷 ☀ 🍁 ❄				

WALK START		DOG WALK CHECKLIST	
WALK END		☐ WASTE BAG	☐ TREAT POUCH
TOTAL WALK		☐ DOG LEASH	☐ WHISTLE
		☐ WATER BOWL	☐ GLOW COLLAR

DOG NAMES & OWNERS

POOP LOG

ROUTE TAKEN	REST STOPS & FOOD

FURTHER NOTES & OBSERVATIONS

LOCATION		DATE
START POINT		
END POINT		/ /

NO. OF DOGS WALKED		WALK RATING	1	2	3	4	5
WEATHER CONDITION	☀ ☁ ❄ ⚡ 💨	TIME OF YEAR	🌷 ☀ 🍃 ❄				

WALK START	🕐	DOG WALK CHECKLIST	
WALK END		☐ WASTE BAG	☐ TREAT POUCH
TOTAL WALK	↻	☐ DOG LEASH	☐ WHISTLE
		☐ WATER BOWL	☐ GLOW COLLAR

DOG NAMES & OWNERS

POOP LOG

ROUTE TAKEN	REST STOPS & FOOD

FURTHER NOTES & OBSERVATIONS

LOCATION		DATE
START POINT		
END POINT		/ /

NO. OF DOGS WALKED		WALK RATING	1	2	3	4	5

WEATHER CONDITION	☀ ☔ ❄ ⛈ 🌬	TIME OF YEAR	🌷 ☀ 🍃 ❄

WALK START	
WALK END	
TOTAL WALK	

DOG WALK CHECKLIST

☐ WASTE BAG ☐ TREAT POUCH
☐ DOG LEASH ☐ WHISTLE
☐ WATER BOWL ☐ GLOW COLLAR

DOG NAMES & OWNERS

POOP LOG

ROUTE TAKEN | REST STOPS & FOOD

FURTHER NOTES & OBSERVATIONS

LOCATION		DATE				
START POINT						
END POINT			/ /			

NO. OF DOGS WALKED		WALK RATING	1	2	3	4	5
WEATHER CONDITION	☀ ☁ ❄ ⛈ 🌬	TIME OF YEAR	🌷 ☀ 🍃 ❄				

WALK START	🕐	**DOG WALK CHECKLIST**	
WALK END		☐ WASTE BAG	☐ TREAT POUCH
TOTAL WALK	↻	☐ DOG LEASH	☐ WHISTLE
		☐ WATER BOWL	☐ GLOW COLLAR

DOG NAMES & OWNERS

POOP LOG

ROUTE TAKEN	REST STOPS & FOOD

FURTHER NOTES & OBSERVATIONS

LOCATION		DATE	
START POINT			
END POINT			

NO. OF DOGS WALKED		WALK RATING	1 2 3 4 5
WEATHER CONDITION	☀ ☁ ❄ ⚡ ≈	TIME OF YEAR	🌷 ☀ 🍃 ❄

WALK START	🕐	**DOG WALK CHECKLIST**	
WALK END		☐ WASTE BAG	☐ TREAT POUCH
TOTAL WALK	↻	☐ DOG LEASH	☐ WHISTLE
		☐ WATER BOWL	☐ GLOW COLLAR

DOG NAMES & OWNERS

POOP LOG

ROUTE TAKEN	REST STOPS & FOOD

FURTHER NOTES & OBSERVATIONS

LOCATION			DATE				
START POINT							
END POINT			/ /				

NO. OF DOGS WALKED			WALK RATING	1	2	3	4	5
WEATHER CONDITION	☀ ☁ ❄ ⚡ 〰		TIME OF YEAR	🌷 ☀ 🍃 ❄				

WALK START	🕐		**DOG WALK CHECKLIST**	
WALK END			☐ WASTE BAG	☐ TREAT POUCH
TOTAL WALK	○		☐ DOG LEASH	☐ WHISTLE
			☐ WATER BOWL	☐ GLOW COLLAR

DOG NAMES & OWNERS

POOP LOG

ROUTE TAKEN / REST STOPS & FOOD

FURTHER NOTES & OBSERVATIONS

LOCATION		DATE	
START POINT			
END POINT		/ /	

NO. OF DOGS WALKED		WALK RATING	1 2 3 4 5
WEATHER CONDITION	☀ ☁ ❄ ⚡ 〰	TIME OF YEAR	🌷 ☀ 🍂 ❄

WALK START		DOG WALK CHECKLIST	
WALK END		☐ WASTE BAG	☐ TREAT POUCH
TOTAL WALK		☐ DOG LEASH	☐ WHISTLE
		☐ WATER BOWL	☐ GLOW COLLAR

DOG NAMES & OWNERS

POOP LOG

ROUTE TAKEN | REST STOPS & FOOD

ROUTE TAKEN	REST STOPS & FOOD

FURTHER NOTES & OBSERVATIONS

LOCATION		DATE
START POINT		
END POINT		/ /

NO. OF DOGS WALKED		WALK RATING	1 2 3 4 5
WEATHER CONDITION	☀ ☁ ❄ ⛈ 🌬	TIME OF YEAR	🌷 ☀ 🍃 ❄

WALK START	🕐	**DOG WALK CHECKLIST**

WALK END		☐ WASTE BAG ☐ TREAT POUCH
TOTAL WALK	↺	☐ DOG LEASH ☐ WHISTLE
		☐ WATER BOWL ☐ GLOW COLLAR

DOG NAMES & OWNERS

POOP LOG

ROUTE TAKEN	REST STOPS & FOOD

FURTHER NOTES & OBSERVATIONS

LOCATION		DATE	
START POINT			
END POINT		/ /	

NO. OF DOGS WALKED		WALK RATING	1	2	3	4	5
WEATHER CONDITION	☀ ☁ ❄ ⛈ 〰	TIME OF YEAR	🌷	☀	🍂	❄	

WALK START	⊕	DOG WALK CHECKLIST	
WALK END		☐ WASTE BAG ☐ TREAT POUCH	
TOTAL WALK	↻	☐ DOG LEASH ☐ WHISTLE	
		☐ WATER BOWL ☐ GLOW COLLAR	

DOG NAMES & OWNERS

POOP LOG

ROUTE TAKEN	REST STOPS & FOOD

FURTHER NOTES & OBSERVATIONS

LOCATION		DATE		
START POINT				
END POINT		/ /		

NO. OF DOGS WALKED		WALK RATING	1	2	3	4	5
WEATHER CONDITION	☀ ☁ ❄ ⛈ 🌬	TIME OF YEAR	🌷 ☀ 🍃 ❄				

WALK START	🕐	DOG WALK CHECKLIST	
WALK END		☐ WASTE BAG	☐ TREAT POUCH
TOTAL WALK	↻	☐ DOG LEASH	☐ WHISTLE
		☐ WATER BOWL	☐ GLOW COLLAR

DOG NAMES & OWNERS

POOP LOG

ROUTE TAKEN	REST STOPS & FOOD

FURTHER NOTES & OBSERVATIONS

LOCATION		DATE	
START POINT			
END POINT			

NO. OF DOGS WALKED		WALK RATING	1 2 3 4 5
WEATHER CONDITION	☀ ☁ ❄ ⛈ 🌬	TIME OF YEAR	🌷 ☀ 🍃 ❄

WALK START	🕐	**DOG WALK CHECKLIST**	
WALK END		☐ WASTE BAG	☐ TREAT POUCH
TOTAL WALK	◯	☐ DOG LEASH	☐ WHISTLE
		☐ WATER BOWL	☐ GLOW COLLAR

DOG NAMES & OWNERS

POOP LOG

ROUTE TAKEN   REST STOPS & FOOD

FURTHER NOTES & OBSERVATIONS

LOCATION		DATE				
START POINT						
END POINT		/	/			

NO. OF DOGS WALKED		WALK RATING	1	2	3	4	5
WEATHER CONDITION	☀ ☁ ❄ ⚡ 🌬	TIME OF YEAR	🌷	☀	🍃	❄	

WALK START	🕐	**DOG WALK CHECKLIST**	
WALK END		☐ WASTE BAG ☐ TREAT POUCH	
TOTAL WALK	🕐	☐ DOG LEASH ☐ WHISTLE	
		☐ WATER BOWL ☐ GLOW COLLAR	

DOG NAMES & OWNERS

POOP LOG

ROUTE TAKEN / REST STOPS & FOOD

FURTHER NOTES & OBSERVATIONS

LOCATION		DATE
START POINT		
END POINT		/ /

NO. OF DOGS WALKED		WALK RATING	1 2 3 4 5
WEATHER CONDITION	☀ ☁ ❄ ⛈ 🌬	TIME OF YEAR	🌷 ☀ 🍃 ❄

WALK START		DOG WALK CHECKLIST	
WALK END		☐ WASTE BAG	☐ TREAT POUCH
TOTAL WALK		☐ DOG LEASH	☐ WHISTLE
		☐ WATER BOWL	☐ GLOW COLLAR

DOG NAMES & OWNERS

POOP LOG

ROUTE TAKEN | REST STOPS & FOOD

FURTHER NOTES & OBSERVATIONS

LOCATION		DATE	
START POINT			
END POINT		/ /	

NO. OF DOGS WALKED		WALK RATING	1 2 3 4 5
WEATHER CONDITION	☀ ☁ ❄ ⛈ 🌬	TIME OF YEAR	🌷 ☀ 🍂 ❄

WALK START	🕐	**DOG WALK CHECKLIST**	
WALK END		☐ WASTE BAG ☐ TREAT POUCH	
TOTAL WALK	↻	☐ DOG LEASH ☐ WHISTLE	
		☐ WATER BOWL ☐ GLOW COLLAR	

DOG NAMES & OWNERS

POOP LOG

ROUTE TAKEN | REST STOPS & FOOD

ROUTE TAKEN	REST STOPS & FOOD

FURTHER NOTES & OBSERVATIONS

LOCATION		DATE	
START POINT			
END POINT			

NO. OF DOGS WALKED		WALK RATING	1 2 3 4 5
WEATHER CONDITION	☀ ☁ ❄ ⚡ 〰	TIME OF YEAR	🌷 ☀ 🍃 ❄

WALK START		DOG WALK CHECKLIST	
WALK END		☐ WASTE BAG ☐ TREAT POUCH	
TOTAL WALK		☐ DOG LEASH ☐ WHISTLE ☐ WATER BOWL ☐ GLOW COLLAR	

DOG NAMES & OWNERS

POOP LOG

ROUTE TAKEN	REST STOPS & FOOD

FURTHER NOTES & OBSERVATIONS

LOCATION		DATE	
START POINT			
END POINT		/	/

NO. OF DOGS WALKED		WALK RATING	1	2	3	4	5
WEATHER CONDITION	☀ ☁ ❄ ⚡ 🌬	TIME OF YEAR	🌷 ☀ 🍃 ❄				

WALK START	🕐	**DOG WALK CHECKLIST**	
WALK END		☐ WASTE BAG	☐ TREAT POUCH
TOTAL WALK	↻	☐ DOG LEASH	☐ WHISTLE
		☐ WATER BOWL	☐ GLOW COLLAR

DOG NAMES & OWNERS

POOP LOG

ROUTE TAKEN · REST STOPS & FOOD

ROUTE TAKEN	REST STOPS & FOOD

FURTHER NOTES & OBSERVATIONS

LOCATION		DATE	
START POINT			
END POINT		/ /	

NO. OF DOGS WALKED		WALK RATING	1	2	3	4	5
WEATHER CONDITION	☀ ☁ ❄ ⛈ 〰	TIME OF YEAR	🌷 ☀ 🍃 ❄				

WALK START		**DOG WALK CHECKLIST**	
WALK END		☐ WASTE BAG	☐ TREAT POUCH
TOTAL WALK		☐ DOG LEASH	☐ WHISTLE
		☐ WATER BOWL	☐ GLOW COLLAR

DOG NAMES & OWNERS

POOP LOG

ROUTE TAKEN / REST STOPS & FOOD

ROUTE TAKEN	REST STOPS & FOOD

FURTHER NOTES & OBSERVATIONS

LOCATION		DATE
START POINT		
END POINT		/ /

NO. OF DOGS WALKED		WALK RATING	1	2	3	4	5

WEATHER CONDITION	☀ ☁ ❄ ⚡ 🌬	TIME OF YEAR	🌷 ☀ 🍃 ❄

WALK START	🕐	DOG WALK CHECKLIST
WALK END		☐ WASTE BAG ☐ TREAT POUCH
TOTAL WALK	⟳	☐ DOG LEASH ☐ WHISTLE
		☐ WATER BOWL ☐ GLOW COLLAR

DOG NAMES & OWNERS

POOP LOG

ROUTE TAKEN	REST STOPS & FOOD

FURTHER NOTES & OBSERVATIONS

LOCATION		DATE
START POINT		
END POINT		/ /

NO. OF DOGS WALKED		WALK RATING	1 2 3 4 5
WEATHER CONDITION		TIME OF YEAR	

WALK START		DOG WALK CHECKLIST	
WALK END		☐ WASTE BAG	☐ TREAT POUCH
TOTAL WALK		☐ DOG LEASH	☐ WHISTLE
		☐ WATER BOWL	☐ GLOW COLLAR

DOG NAMES & OWNERS

POOP LOG

ROUTE TAKEN	REST STOPS & FOOD

FURTHER NOTES & OBSERVATIONS

LOCATION		DATE			
START POINT					
END POINT		/ /			

NO. OF DOGS WALKED		WALK RATING	1	2	3	4	5
WEATHER CONDITION	☀ ☁ ❄ ⛈ 🌬	TIME OF YEAR	🌷 ☀ 🍃 ❄				

WALK START	🕐	DOG WALK CHECKLIST	
WALK END		☐ WASTE BAG ☐ TREAT POUCH	
TOTAL WALK	○	☐ DOG LEASH ☐ WHISTLE	
		☐ WATER BOWL ☐ GLOW COLLAR	

DOG NAMES & OWNERS

POOP LOG

ROUTE TAKEN | REST STOPS & FOOD

ROUTE TAKEN	REST STOPS & FOOD

FURTHER NOTES & OBSERVATIONS

LOCATION		DATE				
START POINT						
END POINT						

NO. OF DOGS WALKED		WALK RATING	1	2	3	4	5
WEATHER CONDITION	☀ ☁ ❄ ⚡ 〰	TIME OF YEAR	🌷	☀	🍃	❄	

WALK START	⏱	DOG WALK CHECKLIST	
WALK END		☐ WASTE BAG ☐ TREAT POUCH	
TOTAL WALK	↻	☐ DOG LEASH ☐ WHISTLE	
		☐ WATER BOWL ☐ GLOW COLLAR	

DOG NAMES & OWNERS

POOP LOG

ROUTE TAKEN / REST STOPS & FOOD

ROUTE TAKEN	REST STOPS & FOOD

FURTHER NOTES & OBSERVATIONS

LOCATION		DATE	
START POINT			
END POINT		/	/

NO. OF DOGS WALKED		WALK RATING	1	2	3	4	5
WEATHER CONDITION	☀ ☁ ❄ ⚡ 〜	TIME OF YEAR	🌷 ☀ 🍃 ❄				

WALK START	🕐	**DOG WALK CHECKLIST**	
WALK END		☐ WASTE BAG	☐ TREAT POUCH
TOTAL WALK	↻	☐ DOG LEASH	☐ WHISTLE
		☐ WATER BOWL	☐ GLOW COLLAR

DOG NAMES & OWNERS

POOP LOG

ROUTE TAKEN	REST STOPS & FOOD

FURTHER NOTES & OBSERVATIONS

LOCATION		DATE		
START POINT				
END POINT		/	/	

NO. OF DOGS WALKED		WALK RATING	1 2 3 4 5
WEATHER CONDITION	☀ ☁ ❄ ⛈ 💨	TIME OF YEAR	🌷 ☀ 🍁 ❄

WALK START	🕐	DOG WALK CHECKLIST	
WALK END		☐ WASTE BAG	☐ TREAT POUCH
TOTAL WALK	↻	☐ DOG LEASH	☐ WHISTLE
		☐ WATER BOWL	☐ GLOW COLLAR

DOG NAMES & OWNERS

POOP LOG

ROUTE TAKEN	REST STOPS & FOOD

FURTHER NOTES & OBSERVATIONS

LOCATION		DATE	
START POINT			
END POINT		/ /	

NO. OF DOGS WALKED		WALK RATING	1 2 3 4 5
WEATHER CONDITION	☀ ☁ ❄ ⚡ 〰	TIME OF YEAR	🌷 ☀ 🍂 ❄

WALK START	🕐	DOG WALK CHECKLIST	
WALK END		☐ WASTE BAG ☐ TREAT POUCH	
TOTAL WALK	🔄	☐ DOG LEASH ☐ WHISTLE	
		☐ WATER BOWL ☐ GLOW COLLAR	

DOG NAMES & OWNERS

POOP LOG

ROUTE TAKEN | REST STOPS & FOOD

FURTHER NOTES & OBSERVATIONS

LOCATION		DATE	
START POINT			
END POINT		/ /	

NO. OF DOGS WALKED		WALK RATING	1 2 3 4 5
WEATHER CONDITION	☀ ☁ ❄ ⚡ 🌬	TIME OF YEAR	🌷 ☀ 🍃 ❄

WALK START		**DOG WALK CHECKLIST**	
WALK END	🕐	☐ WASTE BAG	☐ TREAT POUCH
TOTAL WALK	↻	☐ DOG LEASH	☐ WHISTLE
		☐ WATER BOWL	☐ GLOW COLLAR

DOG NAMES & OWNERS

POOP LOG

ROUTE TAKEN	REST STOPS & FOOD

FURTHER NOTES & OBSERVATIONS

LOCATION		DATE		
START POINT				
END POINT		/	/	

NO. OF DOGS WALKED		WALK RATING	1 2 3 4 5
WEATHER CONDITION	☀ ☁ ❄ ⛈ 🌬	TIME OF YEAR	🌷 ☀ 🍃 ❄

WALK START	🕐	**DOG WALK CHECKLIST**	
WALK END		☐ WASTE BAG	☐ TREAT POUCH
TOTAL WALK	🔄	☐ DOG LEASH	☐ WHISTLE
		☐ WATER BOWL	☐ GLOW COLLAR

DOG NAMES & OWNERS

POOP LOG

ROUTE TAKEN | REST STOPS & FOOD

FURTHER NOTES & OBSERVATIONS

LOCATION		DATE				
START POINT						
END POINT		/ /				

NO. OF DOGS WALKED		WALK RATING	1	2	3	4	5
WEATHER CONDITION	☀ ☁ ❄ ⛈ 🌬	TIME OF YEAR	🌷	☀	🍃	❄	

WALK START		DOG WALK CHECKLIST	
WALK END		☐ WASTE BAG	☐ TREAT POUCH
TOTAL WALK		☐ DOG LEASH	☐ WHISTLE
		☐ WATER BOWL	☐ GLOW COLLAR

DOG NAMES & OWNERS

POOP LOG

ROUTE TAKEN / REST STOPS & FOOD

FURTHER NOTES & OBSERVATIONS

LOCATION		DATE				
START POINT						
END POINT		/	/			

NO. OF DOGS WALKED		WALK RATING	1	2	3	4	5
WEATHER CONDITION	☀ ☁ ❄ ⚡ 🌬	TIME OF YEAR	🌷	☀	🍃	❄	

WALK START	🕐	**DOG WALK CHECKLIST**	
WALK END		☐ WASTE BAG	☐ TREAT POUCH
TOTAL WALK	🔄	☐ DOG LEASH	☐ WHISTLE
		☐ WATER BOWL	☐ GLOW COLLAR

DOG NAMES & OWNERS

POOP LOG

ROUTE TAKEN | REST STOPS & FOOD

ROUTE TAKEN	REST STOPS & FOOD

FURTHER NOTES & OBSERVATIONS

LOCATION		DATE
START POINT		
END POINT		

NO. OF DOGS WALKED		WALK RATING	1 2 3 4 5
WEATHER CONDITION		TIME OF YEAR	

WALK START		**DOG WALK CHECKLIST**	
WALK END		☐ WASTE BAG	☐ TREAT POUCH
TOTAL WALK		☐ DOG LEASH	☐ WHISTLE
		☐ WATER BOWL	☐ GLOW COLLAR

DOG NAMES & OWNERS

POOP LOG

ROUTE TAKEN · REST STOPS & FOOD

FURTHER NOTES & OBSERVATIONS

LOCATION		DATE	
START POINT			
END POINT		/ /	

NO. OF DOGS WALKED		WALK RATING	1 2 3 4 5
WEATHER CONDITION	☀ ☁ ❄ ⚡ 〰	TIME OF YEAR	🌷 ☀ 🍁 ❄

WALK START	🕐	DOG WALK CHECKLIST	
WALK END		☐ WASTE BAG ☐ TREAT POUCH	
TOTAL WALK	↻	☐ DOG LEASH ☐ WHISTLE	
		☐ WATER BOWL ☐ GLOW COLLAR	

DOG NAMES & OWNERS

POOP LOG

ROUTE TAKEN	REST STOPS & FOOD

FURTHER NOTES & OBSERVATIONS

LOCATION		DATE				
START POINT						
END POINT						

NO. OF DOGS WALKED		WALK RATING	1	2	3	4	5
WEATHER CONDITION	☀ ☁ ❄ ⛈ 🌬	TIME OF YEAR	🌷 ☀ 🍃 ❄				

WALK START		DOG WALK CHECKLIST		
WALK END		☐ WASTE BAG	☐ TREAT POUCH	
TOTAL WALK		☐ DOG LEASH	☐ WHISTLE	
		☐ WATER BOWL	☐ GLOW COLLAR	

DOG NAMES & OWNERS

POOP LOG

ROUTE TAKEN	REST STOPS & FOOD

FURTHER NOTES & OBSERVATIONS

LOCATION		DATE				
START POINT						
END POINT						

NO. OF DOGS WALKED		WALK RATING	1	2	3	4	5
WEATHER CONDITION	☀ ☁ ❄ ⚡ 〜	TIME OF YEAR	🌷 ☀ 🍃 ❄				

WALK START	🕐	**DOG WALK CHECKLIST**	
WALK END		☐ WASTE BAG	☐ TREAT POUCH
TOTAL WALK	↻	☐ DOG LEASH	☐ WHISTLE
		☐ WATER BOWL	☐ GLOW COLLAR

DOG NAMES & OWNERS

POOP LOG

ROUTE TAKEN | REST STOPS & FOOD

ROUTE TAKEN	REST STOPS & FOOD

FURTHER NOTES & OBSERVATIONS

LOCATION		DATE
START POINT		
END POINT		/ /

NO. OF DOGS WALKED		WALK RATING	1 2 3 4 5
WEATHER CONDITION	☀ ☁ ❄ ⛈ 🌬	TIME OF YEAR	🌷 ☀ 🍃 ❄

WALK START	🕐	DOG WALK CHECKLIST	
WALK END		☐ WASTE BAG ☐ TREAT POUCH	
TOTAL WALK	🔄	☐ DOG LEASH ☐ WHISTLE	
		☐ WATER BOWL ☐ GLOW COLLAR	

DOG NAMES & OWNERS

POOP LOG

ROUTE TAKEN	REST STOPS & FOOD

FURTHER NOTES & OBSERVATIONS

LOCATION		DATE
START POINT		
END POINT		/ /

NO. OF DOGS WALKED		WALK RATING	1 2 3 4 5
WEATHER CONDITION	☀ ☁ ❄ ⛈ 〰	TIME OF YEAR	🌷 ☀ 🍃 ❄

WALK START	🕐	DOG WALK CHECKLIST	
WALK END		☐ WASTE BAG	☐ TREAT POUCH
TOTAL WALK	↻	☐ DOG LEASH	☐ WHISTLE
		☐ WATER BOWL	☐ GLOW COLLAR

DOG NAMES & OWNERS

POOP LOG

ROUTE TAKEN / REST STOPS & FOOD

ROUTE TAKEN	REST STOPS & FOOD

FURTHER NOTES & OBSERVATIONS

LOCATION		DATE	
START POINT			
END POINT			

NO. OF DOGS WALKED		WALK RATING	1 2 3 4 5
WEATHER CONDITION	☀ ☁ ❄ ⚡ 〰	TIME OF YEAR	🌷 ☀ 🍁 ❄

WALK START		DOG WALK CHECKLIST	
WALK END		☐ WASTE BAG	☐ TREAT POUCH
TOTAL WALK		☐ DOG LEASH	☐ WHISTLE
		☐ WATER BOWL	☐ GLOW COLLAR

DOG NAMES & OWNERS

POOP LOG

ROUTE TAKEN

REST STOPS & FOOD

FURTHER NOTES & OBSERVATIONS

LOCATION		DATE
START POINT		
END POINT		/ /

NO. OF DOGS WALKED		WALK RATING	1 2 3 4 5
WEATHER CONDITION	☀ ☁ ❄ ⚡ 〜	TIME OF YEAR	🌷 ☀ 🍃 ❄

WALK START	🕐	DOG WALK CHECKLIST	
WALK END		☐ WASTE BAG	☐ TREAT POUCH
TOTAL WALK	↻	☐ DOG LEASH	☐ WHISTLE
		☐ WATER BOWL	☐ GLOW COLLAR

DOG NAMES & OWNERS

POOP LOG

ROUTE TAKEN   REST STOPS & FOOD

FURTHER NOTES & OBSERVATIONS

LOCATION		DATE	
START POINT			
END POINT		/ /	

NO. OF DOGS WALKED		WALK RATING	1	2	3	4	5
WEATHER CONDITION	☀ ☔ ❄ ⛈ 🌬	TIME OF YEAR	🌷 ☀ 🍃 ❄				

WALK START		DOG WALK CHECKLIST	
WALK END		☐ WASTE BAG	☐ TREAT POUCH
TOTAL WALK		☐ DOG LEASH	☐ WHISTLE
		☐ WATER BOWL	☐ GLOW COLLAR

DOG NAMES & OWNERS

POOP LOG

ROUTE TAKEN / REST STOPS & FOOD

ROUTE TAKEN	REST STOPS & FOOD

FURTHER NOTES & OBSERVATIONS

_____

LOCATION		DATE		
START POINT				
END POINT		/	/	

NO. OF DOGS WALKED		WALK RATING	1	2	3	4	5

WEATHER CONDITION	☀ ☁ ❄ ⛈ 〜	TIME OF YEAR	🌷 ☀ 🍁 ❄

WALK START	🕐	DOG WALK CHECKLIST	
WALK END		☐ WASTE BAG	☐ TREAT POUCH
TOTAL WALK	○	☐ DOG LEASH	☐ WHISTLE
		☐ WATER BOWL	☐ GLOW COLLAR

DOG NAMES & OWNERS

POOP LOG

ROUTE TAKEN	REST STOPS & FOOD

FURTHER NOTES & OBSERVATIONS

LOCATION		DATE	
START POINT			
END POINT		/ /	

NO. OF DOGS WALKED		WALK RATING	1	2	3	4	5
WEATHER CONDITION	☀ ☁ ❄ ⛈ 🌬	TIME OF YEAR	🌷 ☀ 🍃 ❄				

WALK START	🕐	DOG WALK CHECKLIST	
WALK END		☐ WASTE BAG ☐ TREAT POUCH	
TOTAL WALK	🔄	☐ DOG LEASH ☐ WHISTLE	
		☐ WATER BOWL ☐ GLOW COLLAR	

DOG NAMES & OWNERS

POOP LOG

ROUTE TAKEN | REST STOPS & FOOD

ROUTE TAKEN	REST STOPS & FOOD

FURTHER NOTES & OBSERVATIONS

LOCATION		DATE				
START POINT						
END POINT		/	/			

NO. OF DOGS WALKED			WALK RATING	1	2	3	4	5

WEATHER CONDITION			TIME OF YEAR				

WALK START			**DOG WALK CHECKLIST**		
WALK END			☐ WASTE BAG	☐ TREAT POUCH	
TOTAL WALK			☐ DOG LEASH	☐ WHISTLE	
			☐ WATER BOWL	☐ GLOW COLLAR	

DOG NAMES & OWNERS

POOP LOG

ROUTE TAKEN — REST STOPS & FOOD

FURTHER NOTES & OBSERVATIONS

LOCATION		DATE	
START POINT			
END POINT			

NO. OF DOGS WALKED		WALK RATING	1	2	3	4	5
WEATHER CONDITION	☀ ☁ ❄ ⛈ 💨	TIME OF YEAR	🌷 ☀ 🍃 ❄				

WALK START		**DOG WALK CHECKLIST**	
WALK END		☐ WASTE BAG ☐ TREAT POUCH	
TOTAL WALK		☐ DOG LEASH ☐ WHISTLE	
		☐ WATER BOWL ☐ GLOW COLLAR	

DOG NAMES & OWNERS

POOP LOG

ROUTE TAKEN | REST STOPS & FOOD

FURTHER NOTES & OBSERVATIONS

LOCATION		DATE
START POINT		
END POINT		/ /

NO. OF DOGS WALKED		WALK RATING	1	2	3	4	5
WEATHER CONDITION	☀ ☁ ❄ ⚡ 🌬	TIME OF YEAR	🌷	☀	🍃	❄	

WALK START	🕐	**DOG WALK CHECKLIST**
WALK END		☐ WASTE BAG ☐ TREAT POUCH
TOTAL WALK	🔄	☐ DOG LEASH ☐ WHISTLE
		☐ WATER BOWL ☐ GLOW COLLAR

DOG NAMES & OWNERS

POOP LOG

ROUTE TAKEN	REST STOPS & FOOD

FURTHER NOTES & OBSERVATIONS

LOCATION		DATE	
START POINT			
END POINT		/ /	

NO. OF DOGS WALKED		WALK RATING	1 2 3 4 5
WEATHER CONDITION	☀ ☁ ❄ ⛈ 🌬	TIME OF YEAR	🌷 ☀ 🍃 ❄

WALK START	🕐	DOG WALK CHECKLIST	
WALK END		☐ WASTE BAG	☐ TREAT POUCH
TOTAL WALK	🔄	☐ DOG LEASH	☐ WHISTLE
		☐ WATER BOWL	☐ GLOW COLLAR

DOG NAMES & OWNERS

POOP LOG

ROUTE TAKEN / REST STOPS & FOOD

ROUTE TAKEN	REST STOPS & FOOD

FURTHER NOTES & OBSERVATIONS

LOCATION		DATE			
START POINT					
END POINT		/ /			

NO. OF DOGS WALKED		WALK RATING	1	2 3 4 5
WEATHER CONDITION		TIME OF YEAR		

WALK START		DOG WALK CHECKLIST	
WALK END		☐ WASTE BAG	☐ TREAT POUCH
TOTAL WALK		☐ DOG LEASH	☐ WHISTLE
		☐ WATER BOWL	☐ GLOW COLLAR

DOG NAMES & OWNERS

POOP LOG

ROUTE TAKEN	REST STOPS & FOOD

FURTHER NOTES & OBSERVATIONS

LOCATION		DATE				
START POINT						
END POINT		/ /				

NO. OF DOGS WALKED		WALK RATING	1	2	3	4	5
WEATHER CONDITION	☀ ☁ ❄ ⛈ 💨	TIME OF YEAR	🌷	☀	🍃	❄	

WALK START		DOG WALK CHECKLIST	
WALK END		☐ WASTE BAG	☐ TREAT POUCH
TOTAL WALK		☐ DOG LEASH	☐ WHISTLE
		☐ WATER BOWL	☐ GLOW COLLAR

DOG NAMES & OWNERS

POOP LOG

ROUTE TAKEN

REST STOPS & FOOD

FURTHER NOTES & OBSERVATIONS

LOCATION		DATE
START POINT		
END POINT		/ /

NO. OF DOGS WALKED		WALK RATING	1	2	3	4	5
WEATHER CONDITION	☀ ☁ ❄ ⛈ 🌬	TIME OF YEAR	🌷	☀	🍃	❄	

WALK START	🕐	DOG WALK CHECKLIST		
WALK END		☐ WASTE BAG	☐ TREAT POUCH	
TOTAL WALK	↻	☐ DOG LEASH	☐ WHISTLE	
		☐ WATER BOWL	☐ GLOW COLLAR	

DOG NAMES & OWNERS

POOP LOG

ROUTE TAKEN / REST STOPS & FOOD

ROUTE TAKEN	REST STOPS & FOOD

FURTHER NOTES & OBSERVATIONS

LOCATION		DATE	
START POINT			
END POINT		/ /	

NO. OF DOGS WALKED		WALK RATING	1 2 3 4 5
WEATHER CONDITION	☀ ☁ ❄ ⛈ 🌬	TIME OF YEAR	🌷 ☀ 🍃 ❄

WALK START		DOG WALK CHECKLIST	
WALK END	🕐	☐ WASTE BAG	☐ TREAT POUCH
TOTAL WALK	↻	☐ DOG LEASH	☐ WHISTLE
		☐ WATER BOWL	☐ GLOW COLLAR

DOG NAMES & OWNERS

POOP LOG

ROUTE TAKEN / REST STOPS & FOOD

ROUTE TAKEN	REST STOPS & FOOD

FURTHER NOTES & OBSERVATIONS

LOCATION		DATE
START POINT		
END POINT		/ /

NO. OF DOGS WALKED		WALK RATING	1	2	3	4	5
WEATHER CONDITION	☀ ☁ ❄ ⚡ 🌬	TIME OF YEAR	🌷	☀	🍃	❄	

WALK START	🕐	**DOG WALK CHECKLIST**	
WALK END		☐ WASTE BAG	☐ TREAT POUCH
TOTAL WALK	🔄	☐ DOG LEASH	☐ WHISTLE
		☐ WATER BOWL	☐ GLOW COLLAR

DOG NAMES & OWNERS

POOP LOG

ROUTE TAKEN	REST STOPS & FOOD

FURTHER NOTES & OBSERVATIONS

LOCATION		DATE	
START POINT			
END POINT		/ /	

NO. OF DOGS WALKED		WALK RATING	1	2	3	4	5
WEATHER CONDITION	☀ ☁ ❄ ⚡ ⇒	TIME OF YEAR	🌷 ☀ 🍃 ❄				

WALK START		DOG WALK CHECKLIST	
WALK END		☐ WASTE BAG	☐ TREAT POUCH
TOTAL WALK		☐ DOG LEASH	☐ WHISTLE
		☐ WATER BOWL	☐ GLOW COLLAR

DOG NAMES & OWNERS

POOP LOG

ROUTE TAKEN	REST STOPS & FOOD

FURTHER NOTES & OBSERVATIONS

LOCATION		DATE				
START POINT						
END POINT		/ /				

NO. OF DOGS WALKED		WALK RATING	1	2	3	4	5
WEATHER CONDITION	☀ ☁ ❄ ⛈ 🌬	TIME OF YEAR	🌷	☀	🍂	❄	

WALK START	🕐	DOG WALK CHECKLIST	
WALK END		☐ WASTE BAG ☐ TREAT POUCH	
TOTAL WALK	⟲	☐ DOG LEASH ☐ WHISTLE	
		☐ WATER BOWL ☐ GLOW COLLAR	

DOG NAMES & OWNERS

POOP LOG

ROUTE TAKEN | REST STOPS & FOOD

FURTHER NOTES & OBSERVATIONS

LOCATION		DATE	
START POINT			
END POINT		/ /	

NO. OF DOGS WALKED		WALK RATING	1	2	3	4	5
WEATHER CONDITION	☀ ☁ ❄ ⛈ 🌬	TIME OF YEAR	🌷 ☀ 🍃 ❄				

WALK START	🕐	DOG WALK CHECKLIST	
WALK END		☐ WASTE BAG	☐ TREAT POUCH
TOTAL WALK	⟳	☐ DOG LEASH	☐ WHISTLE
		☐ WATER BOWL	☐ GLOW COLLAR

DOG NAMES & OWNERS

POOP LOG

ROUTE TAKEN	REST STOPS & FOOD

FURTHER NOTES & OBSERVATIONS

LOCATION		DATE	
START POINT			
END POINT		/ /	

NO. OF DOGS WALKED		WALK RATING	1 2 3 4 5
WEATHER CONDITION	☀ ☁ ❄ ⛈ 🌬	TIME OF YEAR	🌷 ☀ 🍃 ❄

WALK START	🕐	DOG WALK CHECKLIST	
WALK END		☐ WASTE BAG	☐ TREAT POUCH
TOTAL WALK	↻	☐ DOG LEASH	☐ WHISTLE
		☐ WATER BOWL	☐ GLOW COLLAR

DOG NAMES & OWNERS

POOP LOG

ROUTE TAKEN / REST STOPS & FOOD

FURTHER NOTES & OBSERVATIONS

LOCATION		DATE	
START POINT			
END POINT		/ /	

NO. OF DOGS WALKED		WALK RATING	1 2 3 4 5
WEATHER CONDITION	☀ ☁ ❄ ⚡ 〰	TIME OF YEAR	❀ ☀ 🍃 ❄

WALK START		DOG WALK CHECKLIST	
WALK END		☐ WASTE BAG	☐ TREAT POUCH
TOTAL WALK		☐ DOG LEASH	☐ WHISTLE
		☐ WATER BOWL	☐ GLOW COLLAR

DOG NAMES & OWNERS

POOP LOG

ROUTE TAKEN	REST STOPS & FOOD

FURTHER NOTES & OBSERVATIONS

LOCATION		DATE
START POINT		
END POINT		/ /

NO. OF DOGS WALKED		WALK RATING	1	2	3	4	5
WEATHER CONDITION	☀ ☁ ❄ ⚡ 🌬	TIME OF YEAR	🌷 ☀ 🍃 ❄				

WALK START	🕐	**DOG WALK CHECKLIST**	
WALK END		☐ WASTE BAG ☐ TREAT POUCH	
TOTAL WALK	🔄	☐ DOG LEASH ☐ WHISTLE	
		☐ WATER BOWL ☐ GLOW COLLAR	

DOG NAMES & OWNERS

POOP LOG

ROUTE TAKEN	REST STOPS & FOOD

FURTHER NOTES & OBSERVATIONS

LOCATION		DATE	
START POINT			
END POINT		/ /	

NO. OF DOGS WALKED		WALK RATING	1 2 3 4 5
WEATHER CONDITION	☀ ☁ ❄ ⚡ 〰	TIME OF YEAR	🌷 ☀ 🍃 ❄

WALK START	🕐	DOG WALK CHECKLIST	
WALK END		☐ WASTE BAG	☐ TREAT POUCH
TOTAL WALK	↻	☐ DOG LEASH	☐ WHISTLE
		☐ WATER BOWL	☐ GLOW COLLAR

DOG NAMES & OWNERS

POOP LOG

ROUTE TAKEN | REST STOPS & FOOD

ROUTE TAKEN	REST STOPS & FOOD

FURTHER NOTES & OBSERVATIONS

Thanks For Reading!

Just a quick message to thank you so much for picking up one of our books! Our sincere hope is that this book has given you the value we always look to provide, and hope we can continue to produce quality books that will in anyway contribute to a better quality of life for our readers.

We are a small independent publisher based in London, UK and we work with talented authors from around the world, who dedicate every ounce of their effort to craft these memorable books for your reading pleasure.

The author of this title would love to hear about your experience with the book, and your review will go a long way to provide them with the insight and encouragement they need to keep creating the kind of books you want to read.

Your Opinion Makes a Real Difference.

If you want to let us know what you thought about the book, please visit the Amazon website and give us your review. We read every single review, no matter how long or short!

Thanks again and until the next time....

HAPPY READING!

Printed in Great Britain
by Amazon